the **Redemption**

Poems by Sera(phina)

Dedication

To You.

And You know very well who You are.

A **Disclaimer**

If you only read the right

You'll only get the end of the story.

If you only read the left

You'll think the story already ended.

This book contains themes of self-harm and suicide. Please read carefully.

I knew how to sing

But

Things got bad

And

My voice hurt.

My voice hurt

And

Things got bad

But

I knew how to sing.

the **mess**

i write when it's too dark to see

the words i scrawl across a page

and when i wake, i close my eyes

so i don't see the mess i made

~~the~~ **~~mess~~**

i write when feelings run me dry

and i scribble all those feelings down

to prove that my arid heart

was nourished with the tears i found

the **ghost**

every time i send her off

she shows up once again

every time i lock her out

i turn to let her in

the ~~ghost~~

every time she comes around

i tell her she should go

she feeds on fear, on hate, on death

those stocks are running low

the **stars**

if it's written in the stars

i surely cannot read their scrawls

or maybe they just lie too far

or maybe they don't care at all

~~the stars~~

few words are written in the stars

but i don't need to read a thing

for i close my eyes, and in the dark

the beauty's there, i hear them sing

Things are always changing,

But

I'm still hurting.

I'm still hurting,

But

Things are always changing.

the **drawing**

sometimes i sketch my darkness
sometimes i make it real
and wonder when it all began
infecting all i feel

when i look at drawings
i drew when i was young
i see the darkness there as well
in all the work i'd done

when did it all start, then?
was i ever really free?
or has the darkness on these pages
always been in me?

~~the~~ **drawing**

i've been sketching once again
after years of letting go
and it's sort of funny what i've seen
when the ink begins to flow

i drew a hero standing in
the castle that she conquered
and i drew gardens, arrayed in hues
without those haunting monsters

these things that i might've drawn
if all hadn't been so dark
the things that time has looked upon
and made a work of art

the **pill**

the pill is small and pink and round

with numbers on the side

i sip a glass of water, swallow

and wonder why they lied

~~the pill~~

it's not like pain has gone away

i still have some tears, some tatters

but it's better now, and people care

i've decided that's what matters

the **chamber**

empty chambers
in the walls
binding my voice
before i call

empty chambers
in the sea
binding my lungs
before i breathe

empty chambers
in the sky
binding my wings
before i fly

empty chambers
in my heart
not binding, but
tearing apart

<s>the</s> <s>**chamber**</s>

empty chambers
giving place
to think aloud
in empty space

empty chambers
giving room
to a find a way
out of my tomb

empty chambers
giving time
to make a better
realer rhyme

empty chambers
giving peace
for in the quiet
i can think

the **death**

at this time, i'm not afraid

of the death and its abyss

really, as far as i'm concerned

it has to be better than this

the ~~death~~

i don't have to be afraid

of the death and what it does

really, as far as i'm concerned

i've already cheated that death once

the **show**

i wait until the darkness comes
when night suffocates the glow
then i swallow up my voice
for the silent evening show

it happens when i'm all alone
when day leaves, then i know
the tears will start to fall quite soon
for the blurry evening show

i sit there on my mattress
'til my cries no longer flow
then i let the pain consume me
for the bloody evening show

~~the show~~

it's calm here in my bedroom
when through the blinds of my window
the sun wakes up the daytime
for the rising morning show

in the early, quiet hours
which knock with such warm glow
i listen to my heart beating
for the gentle morning show

it's not like i forgot those nights
with stains on my pillow
but i can breathe, because it's okay
i know the morning shows

the **family**

"is this your first time?"
the demon says to me
"i swear that you'll love it here"
"this is your family"

"everyone here hates the world"
he went on to say
"you hate it too, you hate it all"
"that's why you can stay"

i look around at everyone
at this family he spoke of
the people who longed to heal
but felt it was too much

the people who ran from death
and trudged back to it again
the sunken eyes, the sallow looks
i guess i'll fit right in

~~the family~~

i tried to return to
my dark and cold domain
but the demon bare his teeth at me
with a dark and cold disdain

"get out," he demanded
"we don't want you here"
"nothing is the same with you"
"not nearly enough fear"

"but i'm sad," i told him
"i think it's back today"
he shook his head and snarled
"i can tell that it won't stay"

"you are no longer like us"
"because you want to fight"
and when i looked around this time
i saw that he was right

I cannot love.

There aren't things

Still worth it.

Love is

Painful.

Painful

Love is

Still worth it.

There aren't things

I cannot love.

the **symptoms**

my face is streaking

my veins are leaking

my hands are shaking

my heart is breaking

my pillow is soaking

my body is choking

my will is bending

my life is ending

~~the symptoms~~

my face is glowing

my veins aren't showing

my hands are holding

what heart's unfolding

my pillow is slept on

my body has kept on

my will is improving

my life is renewing

the **wonder**

they must wonder why i cry

they must think somebody died

but no good reasons have i

for why my face just won't stay dry

the ~~wonder~~

these days, i know why i smile

and why i try to beat those trials

and why, despite my many spirals,

i've chosen, now, to stay a while

the **ocean**

i once saw an ocean
born of all the fears
that people have created
and lived with all these years

an ocean ever deepened
with every brutal war
with every person crucified
with every cry for more

and this darkened ocean
has risen like a flood
widened with the tears of all
reddened with the blood

~~the ocean~~

today i saw an ocean
i nearly dove right in
and let the water cover me
and drag me deep within

but then i felt a drop of water
fall upon my head
and then a hundred thousand more
fall from my eyes instead

the ocean rose a little more
without blood from my veins
today i walked away from death
because i let it rain

the **knife**

i have a knife that i keep close
throughout the good and bad
sometimes i can forget it
sometimes it's all i have

it always seems to be there
clasped right by my side
i never can escape it
i hardly ever try

the knife stays right beside me
in whatever i may do
and one day when i'm buried
it'll be there, too

<s>the</s> **<s>knife</s>**

my hands are too full
my knife no longer fits
i'm overwhelmed by all the things
that darkness can't permit

truth lies within my reach
i'm tightly clutching love
i don't believe what hate made up
i know what i'm made of

that knife, it was too heavy
i could no longer carry it
that knife was indeed buried
but i was alive to bury it

the **debt**

i don't have it bad enough
to justify my sad make-up

i don't own the right excuse
to fund the tears i tend to use

thus, whenever my eyes get wet
i find myself deeper in debt

~~the~~ **~~debt~~**

i don't owe the hearts entombed
an explanation for my wounds

i don't need to make a case
to defend my teary face

i'm not in debt to those who grieve
and if you grieve, you don't owe me

the **thoughts**

my minds moves quicker
than the rest
it races past me
takes my breath

in soiled shadows
it paints a tale
it wants to kill me
it does not fail

i see these images
i cannot fight
they're clear as day
and dark as night

these thoughts will seep
until they burst
i make too many
but they made me first

the thoughts

my mind moves quick
i can't protest
so when it races
i take a breath

i know my thoughts
i know my fears
i know how they got
from there to here

and i know they lie
and i know they steal
and i know they're fake
because i know what's real

and they'll fade away
a shadow always does
i know what they are
they only know who i was

I want to live.

I realize

Things don't always work out,

Though.

Though

Things don't always work out,

I realize

I want to live.

the **marks**

i've fallen in love with

the marks that they leave

because this way, my sadness

will always be believed

~~the~~ **~~marks~~**

i don't need the marks

scattered and growing

i know what i've been through

i know where i'm going

the **million**

i see a million reasons not to try
a million reasons i want to die

a million weapons i could use
a million memories i want to lose

a million nightmares, a million fears
a million thoughts that drove me here

i see a million people who dug my grave
and a single girl they couldn't save

<s>the</s> <s>**million**</s>

i see a million people in their graves
a million mourners where they lay

a million tears to wet the ground
a million more in private bounds

a million hours forever lost
a million choices one would cost

a million moments i might have caved
a million more i'm glad i stayed

the **portraits**

i only want my memories
all colored in the lines
so i ignore the ugly truths
and color in the lies

i want to look back upon
the days pinned to my name
and remember all the smiles
that my eulogy can claim

i want beaming portraits
to line each room and hall
for tears don't look nearly as nice
when hung upon a wall

~~the portraits~~

how could i fall in love with
the hurt that i despised?
how could i see beauty in it?
i guess that i'm surprised

i left behind the searing pain
but i kept the tears i cried
to remind me of how far i've come
from where i might have died

those tears have become portraits
that i'll keep in my archives
they are proof that—even close to death—
i had always been alive

54

the **will**

here's my will, just in case
you don't know what to do
with all the things you uncover
inside my vacant room
        if you find my worries
        just stuff them in a jar
        you might need two or three
        for as many as there are
you'll come across my anger
and underneath, my shame
along with empty boxes
meant for good that never came
        you may not know what to do
        with all the tears you find
        so just pour them in a river
        that doesn't know they're mine
throw out my depression
my nooses and my knives
get rid of all the things
i couldn't get rid of while alive

i have a will, newly revised
it offers better things this time
with souvenirs from all the hills
that i have found a way to climb
        my new will has so much more
        than my old one dared to claim
        beyond the anger, and the hurt
        all the fearing, and the shame
my will talks of fulfillment
and of changes that were good
some tears were left, but healing came
to join them where they stood
        it mentions inspiration
        and a purpose, and a plan
        for everything i cannot do
        it has a hundred that i can
this will is filled with things
that i now can truly give
and it doesn't wait until i die
it is a will to live

the **cut**

if i could just cut the hurt from my life
then i wouldn't need another old knife

if i could just cut out a little more pain
i wouldn't need to touch one more vein

if i could just cut out the failures i saw
i wouldn't cut then, wouldn't cut at all

the ~~cut~~

if i could cut out the pain of my past
cut it all out, cut it at last

if i could just cut the hurt that i felt
leave it behind, the bruises and welts

if could cut out every tear that would fall
i wouldn't do it, wouldn't cut them at all

the **noose**

i can't find my noose
it used to be right here
i must have misplaced it
last time, on the pier

i like to hold that noose
i like to feel its weight
i tie it tight around my neck
fastened to my fate

when i hold that noose
my life is in my hands
i can't control much, yet i
can meet this rope's demands

but where is my noose tonight?
who moved it from my room?
how else am i to prepare
for my impending tomb?

~~the noose~~

it seems my noose has disappeared
where could it have gone?
i haven't moved it in a while
i haven't put it on

i've had so many other things
that i now love to hold
things that don't require
a grave and a scaffold

i guess it could be locked somewhere
by now, i've lost the key
or maybe i just tossed it out
with all my bloody things

that noose could be anywhere
in some corner, in some nook
but i couldn't find that noose today
because today i didn't look

Things were difficult,

Even when

They tried.

They tried

Even when

Things were difficult.

the **breakdown**

i sit down on my mattress

wearing just one shoe

it was abrupt, it made no sense

but it was nothing new

i stare at the window

but i'm not looking through

i don't look out at the sky

but i wonder why it's blue

<s>the</s> **<s>breakdown</s>**

i stand up from my mattress

put my socks on, then my shoes

maybe i move slowly

but at least i can move

some days i feel empty again

and don't know what to do

but i close my eyes and take a breath

i see the sky—it's blue

the **test**

there was a test, i guess, i guess

no one told me about it

because here i am, a mess, a mess

and no one else allows it

~~the~~ ~~test~~

to some degree, i know, i know

we all fail a test or two

but in the end, it shows (it shows)

that failing doesn't break the rules

the **ashes**

fire danced so playfully
coaxing me to go near
i didn't think it hatefully
i didn't think to fear

it all just looked so beautiful
when i watched it from afar
but fire loves to lose control
it loves to make my scars

though the flames were warm
they were so easy to provoke
i didn't think such lovely form
would send me up in smoke

~~the ashes~~

i never thought i'd rise again
from fire's harsh disease
i never thought my burning skin
would ever find release

but all those flames that hurt me
the ones spread from the past
bought purpose from the pain i breathed
brought beauty from the ash

life stirred inside and i awoke
from out of the burning fire
i let the hazy, drifting smoke
just lift me even higher

the **love**

i love the damage, love the harm

love the damage on my arm

love the bandage on it, too

love the damage i can do

~~the love~~

i love the healing in my chest

love the healing of the rest

love the feeling now in me

love the healing that will be

the **numbing**

i can feel my failures like a fire
burning, burning, burning

i can feel the guilt in my belly
churning, churning, churning

i can taste the mistakes on my lips
stirring, stirring, stirring

and the tears trapped in my eyesight
blurring, blurring, blurring

but as i walk this journey, i am
learning, learning, learning

that the numbing of it all is
far, far, more concerning

~~the numbing~~

i can feel my burdens like a weight
lifting, lifting, lifting

i can feel the hatred in my heart
drifting, drifting, drifting

i can feel the anger on my bones
slipping, slipping, slipping

i can feel the rips within my chest
fixing, fixing, fixing

and i know that right now i'm
giving, giving, giving

no more room to numb the pain, i'm
living, living, living

the **limit**

every time i leave the cell

and say that i will free myself

i run into another thing

that easily rebinds my wings

and then i'm back in my prison

knowing just what freedom isn't

the ~~limit~~

i'd been captive—trapped—for years

i'd given up on my frontiers

until i saw i wasn't inside

it was in me all this time

so why should i be prohibited?

my limits themselves are limited

I will continue

Falling

Even though I am

Trying.

I will keep

Collapsing.

I won't keep

Getting up again, though.

I will be on the ground.

I will be on the ground,

Getting up again, though.

I won't keep

Collapsing.

I will keep

Trying.

Even though I am

Falling,

I will continue.

the **water**

no one knows what it's like

at the oceans base

no one knows what lies below

the water on my face

~~the water~~

doesn't matter if they see

what lives within my depths

because i know that way deep down

i have another breath

the **seeing**

she looked happy to anyone
who watched the life she led
but how could they really know
the life inside her head?

she wore a smile that betrayed
the pain hiding instead
from her grin, how could they grasp
the kind of tears she shed?

i wish i'd seen her drowning
in the water that she tread
before she started sinking
in the ocean that she bled

i wish that i had known about
the life inside her head
perhaps, then, she'd not be here
living with the dead

<s>the seeing</s>

someone saw her
with smiles strained
they saw the carvings
of her name

they knew her grief
they felt her pain
they heard the song
her conscience sang

what guilt had streaked
what fear had stained
where life had fled
where tears had rained

someone saw it
what hurt became
someone saw it
and still remained

the **walls**

pain will only change hands

but it won't change at all

it's the story of my life, i know

the writing on the wall

the ~~walls~~

i'm coloring over shameful words

that I have long resented

i'm covering all the dripping lies

with colors I invented

the **regrets**

i can't seem to get to sleep
without writing one more thing
on the dirty, inked up sheet
marked as "my regrets"

then i spend time gambling
with memories that always sting
rewrite them until my eyes leak
and wish i could forget

~~the~~ **regrets**

i could think and think and think
stare at hate, forget to blink
but i've decided i won't sink
with fears that i have met

i won't keep those scribblings
of all the things i hate in me
when times ahead bring better things
why wander in regret?

the **trip**

heartbreak pushed me

out the door

worry drove me

to the airport

anger paid

the ticket's fee

exhaustion led me

to my seat

depression flew

the plane way up

but i was the one

who nearly jumped

~~the~~ ~~trip~~

love talked me

off the ledge

hope coaxed me

to my bed

faith nursed me

back to health

truth told me

about myself

trust began

to heal my hurt

they all agree

my life has worth

the **gray**

on some random, distant day

i woke up to a world of gray

the colors faded, and then they

decided just to stay that way

the ~~gray~~

i feel the morning and its rays

and from the mattress where i lay

i see the colorlessness change

there's a world outside the shades of gray

People expect

More than

I can give.

I can give

More than

People expect.

the **perspective**

i don't see the sun
i see a gun
i don't see life
i see a knife
i don't see hope
i see a rope
i don't see better
i see a goodbye letter
i don't see tomorrow
i see time overdue

+ borrowed

~~the~~ **~~perspective~~**

i don't see hate
i see okay
i don't see hurt
i see worth
i don't see a fight
i see a light
i don't see death
i see one more breath
i don't see the end
i just see beginnings again

+ again

the **mirror**

i hate her, i hate her

why is she here? we both agree

i hate her, i hate her

why is she here, why is she me?

the ~~mirror~~

i see her, i see her

she's not so bad, don't say goodbye

i see her, i'll be her

she's here right now, she's worth the try

the **story**

i tell a story on my arms
i write it on my skin
what others see as bloody harm
i see as life within
              i tell of all the searing pain
              i tell of all the hurt
              dwelling in my bitter veins
              bleeding on my shirt
the voice of blood is louder still
than words drawn from the tongue
stronger than ink, stronger than quill
no need for use of lungs
              because the tumult in my heart
              it comes out in my blood
              all my pain is spilled apart
              in my own crimson flood
my feelings rush with still more strength
when fingers curl to fist
no more breath to speak at length
it's written on my wrist

<s>the **story**</s>

i have a story, just one to tell
my favorite one so far
its history is already spelled
in some old scrapes and scars
   but there is more to talk about
   than gashes will let on
   more is within than is without
   more flows than has been drawn
and more things lie ahead of me
than what lies on my skin
my heart still beats, but this time it's free
to truly beat again
   my scars will fade with time
   but if they choose to stay
   the page that they occupy
   won't be the last page
my story was not just told in pain
some blood i didn't spend
and the best part of it, i maintain
is that it has yet to end

the **dream**

last night, again, i didn't sleep

out of insistent, hateful fear

that waiting underneath the sheets

lies fateful, hateful, mad nightmares

~~the~~ **dream**

last night i really fell asleep

dreamed like i had never dreamed

because nightmares that once plagued me

faltered at my blanket seam

the **gift**

there's only one thing

i know how to give

and just one way out

of the way that i live

~~the gift~~

there's a gift to give

and it's worth so much

and you can ever give it

just never give up

the **anthem**

some broken-record lyrics
against the backdrop of a tune
written in a minor key
sung only to the moon

at the start of my life's episodes
it offers to play again
and my anthem will play once more
when the credits roll

the end.

the ~~anthem~~

there's some broken-record life
that i thought was all i'd get
with my tired little theme song
that spun like a cassette

but i had let myself forget
that i can write songs, too
and they don't play at the end
they play all the way through

to be continued.

Once again,

I find myself

Alone with my tears.

Alone with my tears,

I find myself

Once again.

To Whoever Needs It—

Things get better. They do. You've probably heard it before. But I mean it. It can be hard, and it can hurt. And sometimes there's an obvious reason for the pain, and sometimes there really isn't any articulate reason at all. It's okay, you know. You're allowed to feel it, the tightness in your chest and the thickness of your throat and the tears, whether they're wet or dry. Sometimes, you might not be able to feel anything, and that can be unsettling. But it will pass. It will pass, again and again. Ask for help if you need it. I know that you might feel like a burden sometimes, but believe me, there *are* people who *want* to help you. And it will be okay. I promise you, it's worth it.

Love,
Sera(phina)